SPACE MYSTERIES

HOW BIG IS THE UNIVERSE?

Gareth Stevens
PUBLISHING

BY MATT JANKOWSKI

Please visit our website, www.garethstevens.com. For a free color catalog of all our high-quality books, call toll free 1-800-542-2595 or fax 1-877-542-2596.

Cataloging-in-Publication Data

Names: Jankowski, Matt.
Title: How big is the universe? / Matt Jankowski.
Description: New York : Gareth Stevens Publishing, 2019. | Series: Space mysteries | Includes index.
Identifiers: LCCN ISBN 9781538219492 (pbk.) | ISBN 9781538219478 (library bound) | ISBN 9781538219508 (6 pack)
Subjects: LCSH: Astronomy--Juvenile literature. | Cosmology--Juvenile literature.
Classification: LCC QB46.J36 2018 | DDC 520--dc23

First Edition

Published in 2019 by
Gareth Stevens Publishing
111 East 14th Street, Suite 349
New York, NY 10003

Copyright © 2019 Gareth Stevens Publishing

Designer: Katelyn E. Reynolds
Editor: Joan Stoltman

Photo credits: Cover, p. 1 NASA (http://www.nasa.gov/), ESA (http://www.spacetelescope.org/), H. Teplitz and M. Rafelski (IPAC/Caltech), A. Koekemoer (STScI (http://www.stsci.edu/), R. Windhorst (Arizona State University), and Z. Levay (STScI (http://www.stsci.edu/); cover, pp. 1, 3–32 (background texture) David M. Schrader/Shutterstock.com; pp. 3–32 (fun fact graphic) © iStockphoto.com/spxChrome; p. 5 NASA/Tony Gray and Sandra Joseph; pp. 7, 29 NASA; p. 9 (inset) David J Wilson/Wikipedia.org; p. 9 (main) Corbis Documentary/Getty Images; p. 11 NASA/JPL-Caltech/ T. Pyle (SSC); p. 13 NASA's Goddard Space Flight Center/S. Wiessinger; p. 15 NASA/JPL-Caltech; p. 17 WIN-Initiative/ Getty Images; p. 19 Vilde Indrehus/Moment/Getty Images; p. 20 NASA/JPL-Caltech/L. Jenkins (GSFC); p. 21 NASA, ESA, Jennifer Lotz and the HFF Team (STScI); p. 23 NASA/JPL; p. 25 (top) Gabe Ginsberg/WireImage/Getty Images; p. 25 (bottom) Andrew Burton/Getty Images News/Getty Images; p. 27 Subaru/NASA/JPL-Caltech.

Printed in the United States of America

CPSIA compliance information: Batch #CS18GS: For further information contact Gareth Stevens, New York, New York at 1-800-542-2595.

CONTENTS

Words in the glossary appear in **bold** type the first time they are used in the text.

UNIVERSALLY KNOWN

To find out how big the universe is, you'll first need to know *what* the universe is! The universe is all of outer space—including every single star, **planet**, moon, **galaxy**, and more! In other words, the universe is everything that exists.

It's hard to picture the size of the universe because it's made up of everything! Figuring out the size of galaxies, planets, and other objects in outer space helps us make sense of just how huge the universe is.

Right now, only **astronauts** can go to space, but pretty soon, anyone with enough money may be able to travel there! In the meantime, a good way to go out of this world is to use your imagination and read books about space!

GREETINGS, EARTHLING!

You might have some idea about Earth's size. You likely even have an idea of the size of your city, state, and country. You may know about how big your **continent** is.

The Earth is about 25,000 miles (40,235 km) around. If you were going 50 miles (80 km) per hour in a car and could drive across oceans, it would take you over 20 days to circle back to where you started!

OUT OF THIS WORLD!

Oceans cover over 70 percent of Earth's surface. The largest ocean is the Pacific Ocean—which is almost the size of all land on Earth combined!

This is a picture of what Earth looks like from space!
You can see that oceans cover a large amount of our planet.

A REVOLUTIONARY CONCEPT

Long ago, people believed Earth was the center of the universe. They saw the sun come up every morning and go down every night and decided Earth must stay still and everything in space must move around it. It turns out they were very wrong!

A scientist named Galileo Galilei started to look more closely at the night sky using a telescope. He realized Earth was actually moving—in fact, Earth was **revolving** around the sun!

OUT OF THIS WORLD!

Thanks to Galileo, we also know that the Earth **rotates** every 24 hours. Daytime is when the part of Earth you live on is facing, or rotated toward, the sun. Nighttime is when it's rotated away from the sun!

A telescope is a long, tube-shaped tool that makes faraway things look closer. The telescopes of Galileo's time were very simple. Today, telescopes are very powerful!

9

HERE COMES THE SUN

From our homes here on Earth, the sun looks like a small, warm, bright ball of fire. If you went to space, however, you would discover the sun is actually huge!

The sun makes Earth and all the planets in our **solar system** move around it. This kind of movement is called orbiting. Because the sun is so much bigger than the planets, a force called **gravity** exists between the sun and planets to keep them in orbit.

OUT OF THIS WORLD!

The sun is the size of over 1 million Earths. It's also the size of about 1,000 Jupiters, the biggest planet in our solar system!

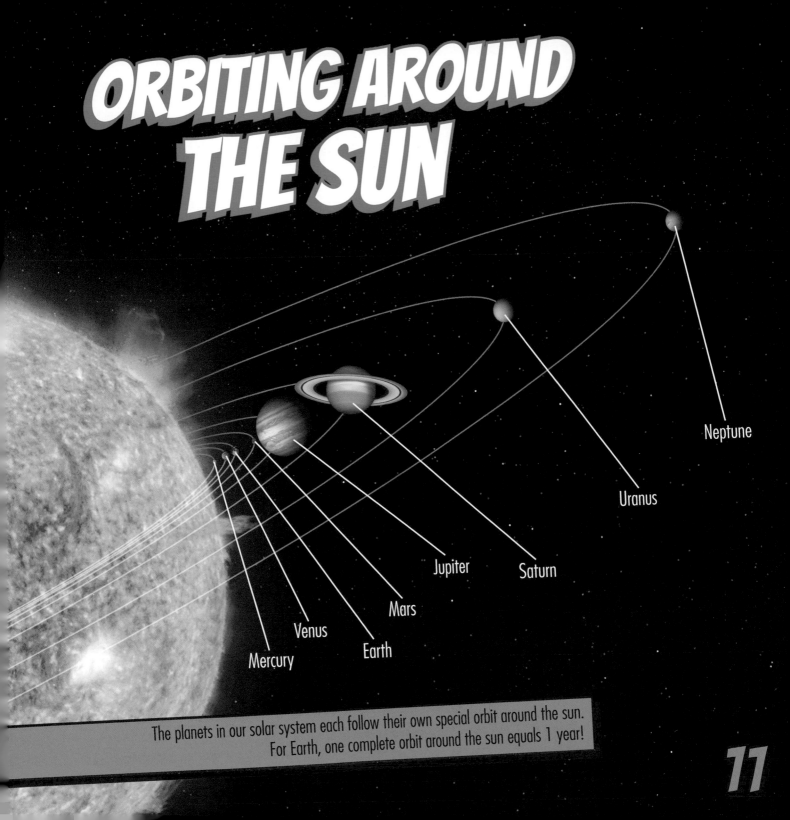

ORBITING AROUND THE SUN

Neptune

Uranus

Jupiter   Saturn

Mars

Venus

Earth

Mercury

The planets in our solar system each follow their own special orbit around the sun.
For Earth, one complete orbit around the sun equals 1 year!

11

STARRY, STARRY NIGHT

From Earth, stars only look small because we're so far away from them. The sun looks like the largest star to us, but that's only because it's the closest to us!

The sun is a yellow dwarf star. Yellow dwarf stars are in the middle in terms of how big or small stars can be. They're bigger than red dwarf stars, but smaller than giant stars. Red giant and blue giant stars can be 100 to 1,000 times bigger than our sun!

OUT OF THIS WORLD!

The biggest giant stars are called supergiants, and they're very **rare**! They can be several hundred times wider than our sun!

This blue supergiant star is about 864 million miles (1.4 billion km) across! That's almost 1,000 times larger than our sun!

Our Sun

SOLAR SYSTEMS

Our solar system is made up of the sun and eight planets. "Solar" means "having to do with the sun." Every solar system in the universe has a sun in the center. You didn't think there was only one solar system in the whole universe, did you?

Scientists don't know exactly how many solar systems there are, but they guess there could be up to 100 billion in our galaxy alone. Some are bigger, and some are smaller than our galaxy!

OUT OF THIS WORLD!

A galaxy is a large group of planets, gas, dust, and billions of stars that form a group within the universe. Our galaxy is called the Milky Way.

← Our Solar System

Our solar system is just a small part of the Milky Way galaxy, which is itself a small part of the universe! As you can see, there are plenty of stars for other solar systems to form around.

HOW MANY?!

The Milky Way galaxy not only has up to 100 billion solar systems, but it also has 100 billion planets and 100 to 400 billion stars. And that's just one galaxy! Scientists think there could be at least 2,000 billion galaxies in the universe!

The Andromeda galaxy is the closest major galaxy to our own. Scientists think it may have 1,000 billion stars! Andromeda is the largest of the 54 galaxies in the Local Group, which is the set of galaxies nearest us.

OUT OF THIS WORLD!

The best time to see the Andromeda galaxy is in early October around midnight. **Binoculars** can help!

Here's what the Milky Way galaxy looks like from Earth.

LIGHT-YEARS AWAY

The universe is far too big to measure in miles, so scientists use light-years. Light-years sound as if they could be a measurement for time, but they actually measure distance.

A light-year equals the distance that light travels in 1 year, which is around 5.88 trillion miles (9.46 trillion km). The speed of light is 186,000 miles (299,000 km) per second. If you could travel at the speed of light, you'd be able to circle Earth about 7.5 times in 1 second!

By the time a star's light travels to Earth
for us to see, that star may already be dead!

GALAXY CLUSTERS

Galaxies may be pulled together by gravity into groups called clusters. The Local Group is a cluster about 10 million light-years across that contains more than 30 galaxies. Some clusters are much larger. The Coma Cluster contains thousands of galaxies and is over 20 million light-years across!

The gravitational pull of a cluster may be strong enough to attract other clusters. When this happens, a supercluster is formed!

Coma Cluster

This is a picture of galaxy cluster Abell 370 taken from a space telescope. Abell 370 is 4 billion light-years away from Earth. Each spiral in the picture is a separate galaxy within Abell 370.

SATELLITES

Other solar systems, galaxies, and clusters are millions of light-years away, but humans have only traveled as far as the moon. So how do we know so much about the universe? Much of our knowledge comes from satellites—machines that travel into space to take pictures and collect **data**.

Astronomy satellites orbit Earth. Space exploration satellites are actually probes. A probe is an object that's been built to travel into deep space and send data back. Some satellites even have powerful telescopes!

OUT OF THIS WORLD!

The Hubble Space Telescope is an astronomy satellite that was sent into space in 1990 by NASA (National Aeronautics and Space Administration). Pictures from the Hubble Space Telescope have provided much of what we now know about space.

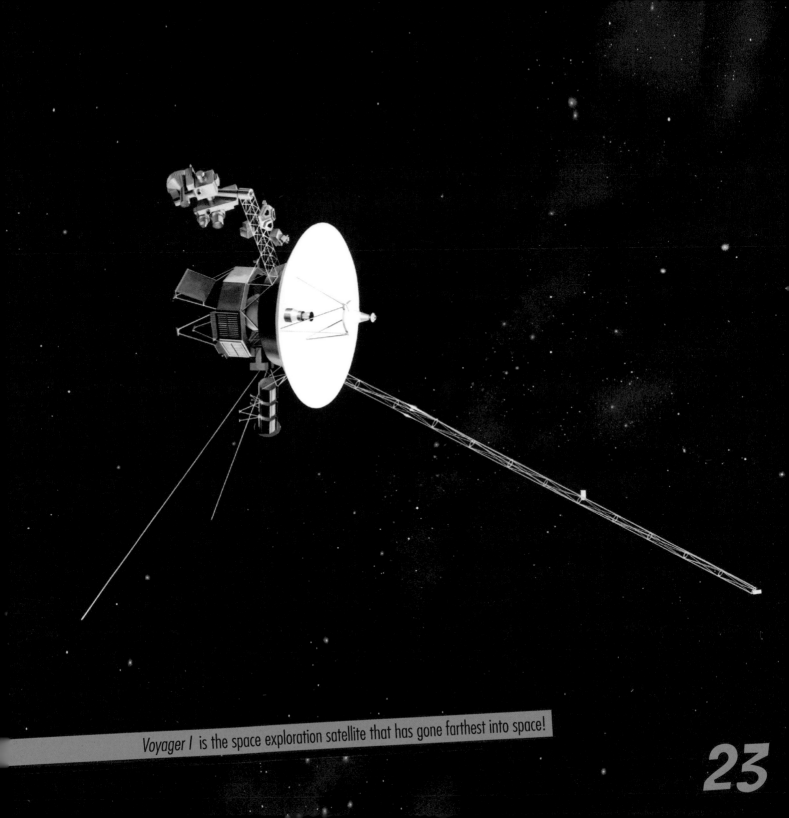

Voyager I is the space exploration satellite that has gone farthest into space!

23

BUT HOW BIG IS IT?

So, we know that our sun is pretty small compared to other stars. We also know that many other stars have their own solar systems and that there may be billions of solar systems in each galaxy. Clusters of galaxies can have thousands of galaxies in them and are so big they're measured in light-years.

We know all this thanks to the data from space satellites! But have scientists been able to figure out how big the universe is?

OUT OF THIS WORLD!

Some books and movies that are known as science fiction, or sci-fi, take place in outer space.

FROM DIRECTOR JUSTIN LIN AND PRODUCER J.J. ABRAMS

STAR TREK
BEYOND

IN REAL D 3D AND IMAX 3D

SKYDANCE 07.22.16 StarTrekMovie.com

STAR WARS
THE FORCE AWAKENS

IS THAT YOUR FINAL ANSWER?

Scientists still don't know exactly how big the universe is! They estimate, or guess using data, that the universe is about 13.8 billion years old. That means the universe must be 13.8 billion light-years across, right? It's not quite that simple.

It means any light we see has traveled for 13.8 billion years or less. However, since the universe is always expanding, or growing bigger, scientists estimate the universe may be 46 billion light-years wide!

OUT OF THIS WORLD!

In the time you've been reading this book, the universe has grown bigger!

This is a picture of a cluster of young galaxies forming.
The universe is much too large to capture in a single picture.

THE FINAL FRONTIER

Outer space doesn't seem that far away from Earth because all we have to do is look up. But, as it turns out, the stars we can see are light-years away—and there are many more stars we can't see. If you're struggling to picture in your head how big the universe is, you're not alone. Scientists have the same struggle!

The only thing we're sure of is that the universe is huge and always growing!

OUT OF THIS WORLD!

NASA scientists are trying to find answers to many questions about space. Can humans reach Mars? Is there life on other planets?

This astronaut waves while fixing part of the Hubble Space Telescope.

GLOSSARY

astronaut: someone who works or lives in space

astronomy: the science of stars and other objects in outer space

binoculars: a tool that you hold up to your eyes and look through to see faraway objects

continent: one of Earth's seven great landmasses

data: facts and figures

galaxy: a large group of stars, planets, gas, and dust that form a group within the universe

gravity: the force that pulls objects toward the center of a planet or star

planet: a large, round object in space that travels around a star

rare: uncommon or special

revolve: to turn around a center point or line

rotate: to move or turn in a circle

solar system: a star and all the space objects that orbit it, including planets and their moons

FOR MORE INFORMATION

BOOKS

Aldrin, Buzz, and Marianne J. Dyson. *Welcome to Mars: Making a Home on the Red Planet*. Washington, DC: National Geographic, 2015.

Hughes, Catherine D. *First Big Book of Space*. Washington, DC: National Geographic, 2012.

Rao, Joe. *Looking Up! The Science of Stargazing*. New York, NY: Simon Spotlight, 2017.

WEBSITES

HubbleSite
hubblesite.org/
Look at pictures and watch videos of the stars and galaxies taken by the Hubble Space Telescope.

NASA Space Place
spaceplace.nasa.gov/
Visit this website to learn about Earth and outer space while playing games, watching movies, and much more!

Space Scoop
www.spacescoop.org/en/
This site makes news from the top space programs into articles that are easy for kids to read!

INDEX